Web Application with Spring Annotation-Driven Configuration

By Juliano Alves Cassoli

Table of Contents

Preface

Spring Framework is an open source application framework created to provide infrastructure support for developing Java applications and it's the central point of our practical journey in this book. Around it, we will cover the use of its tools integrated with web applications and some of the framework key features to achieve fast and robust results on development process. We also will be using other tools like Maven to build, deploy and keep dependencies in the example code, Hibernate to manage persistence and the ultimate Spring Data JPA mechanism. It is assumed you already have Java 8 basic programming skills and knows at least the basics of a Web Server, Servlet container and Servlet specification 3+, as well as the basics of ORM and relational data bases.

I've been working with java and web application using Spring framework for quite sometime, since version 2.x with configurations done with plenty XML files and then versions 3.x that, not just introduced a strong Java 5+ foundations across the framework codebase, but the so called Java-based configuration model and this is the focus of the solutions presented here. This is a short but concise compilation of my experience building applications with the latest version of spring.

I must confess I have never been a big fan of XML configurations when it comes to frameworks, even in my experiences working with EJB 2.x, which is heavily configured with XML, or Struts in its early versions, I thought was a bad idea to spend so many hours on complicated and extensive XML files because it is too verbose and susceptible to failure. Besides, XML files are poorly assisted in development environments, for one simple reason, they are not the target purpose of those environments, which of course is the programming language. Java is type safe, compiler will report problems, you have tools like code assist and completion, therefore it's a so much cleaner and easier way to customize your initialization using mechanisms like Annotations, Interfaces and package scanning, and either you can directly use the programming resources of the framework, instead of guessing how to invoking them textually in the XML.

This book is intended to be used as a fast reference for any programmer who needs code snippets to solve their specific day-by-day problems or assistance to integrate spring with existent Java Web Application by giving explained situations with code examples. We will be using Spring framework version 4.3, Tomcat 8, Java 8, Hibernate 5.1 among other components presented through the Chapters.

"Readiness is all" – William Shakespeare

Chapter 1. Preparing your Environment

In the subsequent chapters there will be example code illustrating the topics with tools like Eclipse and Tomcat, if you are not so familiar with it and you intend to execute those examples, it will be better and more comfortable to setup an environment following this step-by-step.

Java Platform

This book is not intended to teach you the Java language, but if you are starting to know the java platform I believe this book can help you to get in touch with a practical use of such widely known framework as Spring.

Eclipse

You can produce your code with any text editor but it will be so much harder not using an IDE. In many books out there, the authors try to be simplistic and therefore adopt poor tools, but this is not the case, you will find the examples ready to run using Eclipse. If you already have your environment set you can pass this chapter of course, but if you don't, and are at least expecting suggestions, see the following instructions get the same environment I use for my projects.

You should get Eclipse IDE for Java EE Developers. At the time I am writing this, the latest version of Eclipse is "Neon Release (4.6.0)", go to the download page and get the right version for your system:

http://www.eclipse.org/downloads/packages/eclipse-ide-java-ee-developers/neonr

The EE version has many tools you are going to use on your web application. I recommend you do download the ZIP version and unzip it in a common development environment folder, if you are using Windows you can create a folder like this: "`c:\development`", and then you will have this path: "`C:\development\eclipse`".

Apache Tomcat

The context of this book is web applications, so we will need a runtime – a web server and servlet container – suitable for adoption of spring framework, that's why we will be using Apache Tomcat 8. Download the ZIP version just like you did with Eclipse and unzip it on development folder, again assuming you are using Windows.

http://tomcat.apache.org/download-80.cgi

Following my directions, you will have this "`C:\development\apache-tomcat-8.5.4`".

Persistence

To run the examples with Spring Data JPA and integration with Hibernate, you will need to have a relational data base running, I recommend you to install MySQL, the community server is for free:

https://www.mysql.com/

MySQL offers a very good tool to operate the data base, list tables, registers and manipulate the data, it is the MySQL Workbench, you can download it here:

https://dev.mysql.com/downloads/workbench/

There are another set of tools that can help you, a simpler one compared to Workbench but it's discontinued by the MySQL team. It still works and personally I think it's still very useful, it is called MySQL GUI Tools:

https://downloads.mysql.com/archives/gui/

Plugins for Eclipse

After you get Eclipse running, let's configure the Java JDK as default Installed JRE, I usually do this to avoid some problems when I configure servers which needs access to JDK instead of JRE. In the Eclipse menu bar, select `Window -> Preferences`, then find `Java -> Installed JREs` on the left pane. Make the JDK the default as seen here:

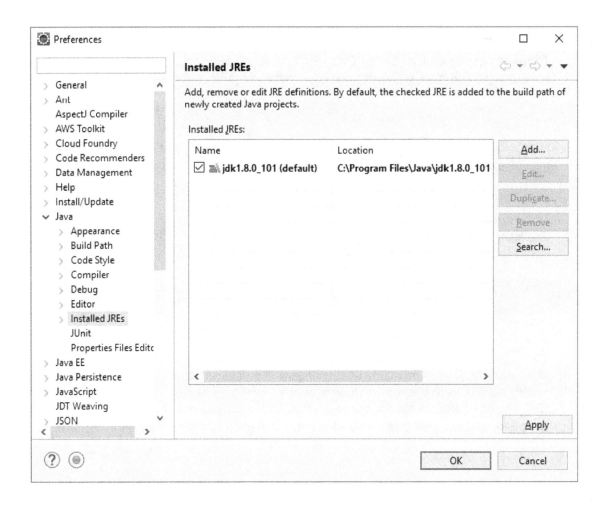

We need to add and setup the Tomcat in `Servers`, access the Servers View to create new server, if you don't see it, then go to `Window -> Show View -> Servers` and you will see this:

Click to create a server, select Apache and `Tomcat v8.0 Server` as seen below

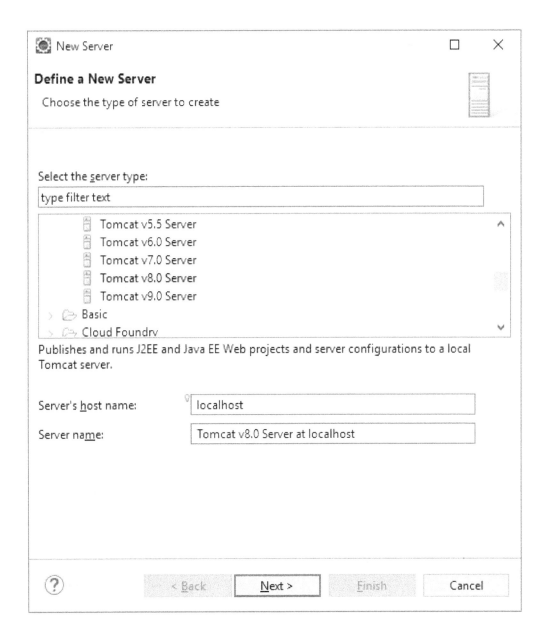

Once the server is ok, let's move forward and install some helpful plugins. The Spring IDE is a very good one with many interesting tools and a viewer for artifacts, can be found here:

https://marketplace.eclipse.org/content/spring-ide

Configuring Spring Plugin

If you start a Dynamic Web Project in Eclipse and add Spring to it (even by adding the jar files on WEB-INF/lib or adding dependencies in the POM), you will notice that it is not automatically recognizable as a Spring project by the plugin you've installed, you will have it to tell it to Eclipse. Right-click your project and select `Spring Tools -> Add Spring Project Nature` as seen below:

And you see some changes like a little "S" on the project icon and a little green leaf titled "Spring Elements" as part of you project items seen here:

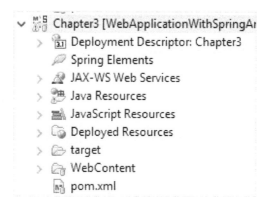

This "Spring Elements" is meant to show you many elements and settings items found on your project, but as you can see it is apparently empty, why? It's because the plugin was designed initially to get your Spring configuration by XML. To get it running with the programmatic annotation-driven configuration covered in this book, you will have to indicate the configuration class it must look to build the element viewer. Right-click the project and select `Preferences`, then go to `Spring -> Beans Support` and you will see this dialog:

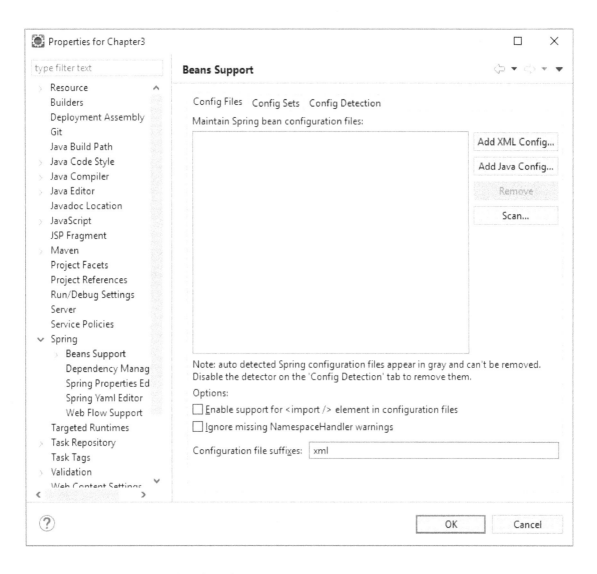

Now click "Add Java Config..." or Click "Scan..." and select your classes annotated with @Configuration, or simply select your main configuration class. If it loads the configuration properly you will see the components like this:

If you don't want to install The Spring Plugin, I think you should consider install this one: The Quick Search

Eclipse Quick Search is a fast and easy to use "search as you type" text search tool. Open with Cmd-Shift-L, type your search and see results immediately.

https://marketplace.eclipse.org/content/quick-search-eclipse

Maven

And the last but not least, the Maven plugin.

http://www.eclipse.org/m2e/

This one is important, not just because all the example code we will discuss is integrated with Maven but it's also a great tool to have in your projects. The plugin makes a very good integration with Eclipse and give so many facilities to you with the following features (described in the web site):

Launching Maven builds from within Eclipse
Dependency management for Eclipse build path based on Maven's pom.xml
Resolving Maven dependencies from the Eclipse workspace without installing to local Maven repository
Automatic downloading of the required dependencies from the remote Maven repositories
Wizards for creating new Maven projects, pom.xml and to enable Maven support on plain Java project
Quick search for dependencies in Maven remote repositories

If you don't know much about it, you should take a look:

Maven...
...is a tool that can now be used for building and managing any Java-based project. We hope that we have created something that will make the day-to-day work of Java developers easier and generally help with the comprehension of any Java-based project.

Making the build process easy
Providing a uniform build system
Providing quality project information
Providing guidelines for best practices development
Allowing transparent migration to new features

You can get more information at:

https://maven.apache.org/

With Maven we will have a file named pom.xml which stands for Project Object Model, see what the maven project web site says:

A Project Object Model or POM is the fundamental unit of work in Maven. It is an XML file that contains information about the project and configuration details used by Maven to build the project.
...
When executing a task or goal, Maven looks for the POM in the current directory. It reads the POM, gets the needed configuration information, then executes the goal.

Some of the configuration that can be specified in the POM are the project dependencies, the plugins or goals that can be executed, the build profiles, and so on. Other information such as the project version, description, developers, mailing lists and such can also be specified.

In the examples of this book I will show you how to configure your POM to run what is presented in each Chapter.

GitHub

All the examples can be found to download freely on GitHub, a service based on Git version control system. You don't even need to make an account to download the examples, see:

https://github.com/

The examples can be cloned into Eclipse by accessing the projects page at GitHub (given at the end of each chapter), coping the appropriate URL link entitled "Clone with HTTPS" and then select `File -> Import -> Projects from GIT`.

Or if you are downloading the projects outside Eclipse, you can simply add them to the environment by going to menu `File -> Import -> Existing Projects into Workspace`.

Chapter 2. Application Startup and Initialization

If we want to build a configuration to integrate Spring, we must do it to run when the server starts the execution of the application. After the application has been deployed the servlet container will create a mapping context to the web application and then produce some events that can be captured by event listeners.

Thanks to the `ServletContainerInitializer` API added to Servlet 3.0, in this initial phase Tomcat will scan packages to find implementations of the interface `ServletContainerInitializer` annotated with `HandleTypes`, in order to receive at its "onStartup" method the Set of application classes that implement, extend, or have been annotated with the class types specified by the annotation. See JSR for Servlet 3.1 snippet below:

> Application event listeners are classes that implement one or more of the servlet event listener interfaces. They are instantiated and registered in the Web container at the time of the deployment of the Web application. They are provided by the Developer in the WAR.
>
> Servlet event listeners support event notifications for state changes in the ServletContext, HttpSession and ServletRequest objects. Servlet context listeners are used to manage resources or state held at a JVM level for the application. HTTP session listeners are used to manage state or resources associated with a series of requests made into a Web application from the same client or user.

We don't need to get deeper in to the details of the implementation of the container but it's enough to understand that Tomcat has a mechanism to build hookups to its events at startup by the interface `ServletContainerInitializer` with `HandleTypes` and that's what Spring uses through a class named `SpringServletContainerInitializer` and indicating on the annotation the interface `WebApplicationInitializer`. In other words, if you want to have your application initializer, create an implementation of `WebApplicationInitializer` and then Tomcat will execute it as soon as your application is loaded. See the code snippet below:

```
import javax.servlet.ServletContext;
import javax.servlet.ServletException;

import org.apache.logging.log4j.LogManager;
import org.apache.logging.log4j.Logger;
import org.springframework.web.WebApplicationInitializer;
```

```java
/**
 * @author Juliano Cassoli
 *
 */
public class MyAppInitializer implements
WebApplicationInitializer {

    private static final Logger logger =
LogManager.getLogger(MyAppInitializer.class);

    @Override
    public void onStartup(ServletContext servletContext)
throws ServletException {

        // Some useful information
        logger.info("Your Application version 1.0.0");
        logger.info("OS: " + System.getProperty("os.name")
+ ", version " + System.getProperty("os.version")
            + ", Archtecture " +
System.getProperty("os.arch"));
        logger.info("Processors: " +
Runtime.getRuntime().availableProcessors());


    }

}
```

Logging

Right at the beginning of the class we can see the attribute statement to get Logger from Log4j, this is important, if you do System out print calls in your code you should stop doing this, it is a non-professional, bad practice for a number of reasons, `System.out.println` calls are IO blocking operations and therefore time consuming (your program wait until println has finished), when your application goes in production you can't separate it from the server's log, you cannot determine levels of messages - if they are critical or just information. With Log4j you can create a pattern and format your message setting useful information, also you can configure a log file policy and don't end up having your server run out of disk with a giant log file. In this book we will be using log4j version 2 which is suitable for Servlets 3.0+.

If you are planning to run this examples in tomcat 7, there is a very important thing to consider when using Log4j 2 and that's why I recommend using Tomcat 8, from the documentation of Log4j 2:

Important Note! For performance reasons, containers often ignore certain JARs known not to contain TLDs or ServletContainerInitializers and do not scan them for web-fragments and initializers. Importantly, Tomcat 7 <7.0.43 ignores all JAR files named log4j*.jar, which prevents this feature from working. This has been fixed in Tomcat 7.0.43, Tomcat 8, and later. In Tomcat 7 <7.0.43 you will need to change catalina.properties and remove "log4j*.jar" from the jarsToSkip property. You may need to do something similar on other containers if they skip scanning Log4j JAR files.

When working with Tomcat, one of the main reasons you should not call system output is that all your messages will go to a file named "catalina.out", in Windows you won't have problems with this but in Linux flavors I've seen production servers run out of disk because of that. To avoid this problem what I do is to have 2 Log4j configuration files, one to be used in production environment and another that will be loaded in development at runtime, lets first take a look at the development one, I call it "log4j2-dev.xml":

```xml
<?xml version="1.0" encoding="UTF-8"?>
<Configuration status="ERROR">
      <Properties>
            <property name="log-
path">${sys:user.home}/logs</property>
            <property name="log-
name">WASADC_Chapter2</property>
      </Properties>
  <Appenders>
    <Console name="Console" target="SYSTEM_OUT">
      <PatternLayout pattern="%d %5p (%F:%L) - %m%n"/>
    </Console>
    <RollingFile name="RollingFile" fileName="${log-
path}/${log-name}.log"
                  filePattern="${log-path}/$${date:yyyy-
MM}/${log-name}-%d{MM-dd-yyyy}-%i.log.gz">
      <PatternLayout>
        <Pattern>%d %5p (%F:%L) - %m%n</Pattern>
      </PatternLayout>
      <Policies>
        <TimeBasedTriggeringPolicy />
        <SizeBasedTriggeringPolicy size="10 MB"/>
      </Policies>
      <DefaultRolloverStrategy max="5"/>
    </RollingFile>
  </Appenders>
  <Loggers>
    <Root level="debug">
```

```
        <AppenderRef ref="Console"/>
        <AppenderRef ref="RollingFile"/>
    </Root>
  </Loggers>
</Configuration>
```

It's a very simple configuration but does all you need. It will create (and concatenate messages) in a file at your home user /logs, will keep your file with 10 MB at most and roll over 5 zipped files deleting the older one. Also it will send messages to console, in Eclipse this is very useful. Now this is my production configuration:

```
<?xml version="1.0" encoding="UTF-8"?>
<Configuration status="ERROR">
      <Properties>
            <property name="log-
path">${sys:user.home}/logs</property>
            <property name="log-
name">WASADC_Chapter2</property>
      </Properties>
  <Appenders>
    <RollingFile name="RollingFile" fileName="${log-
path}/${log-name}.log"
                 filePattern="${log-path}/$${date:yyyy-
MM}/${log-name}-%d{MM-dd-yyyy}-%i.log.gz">
      <PatternLayout>
        <Pattern>%d %5p (%F:%L) - %m%n</Pattern>
      </PatternLayout>
      <Policies>
        <TimeBasedTriggeringPolicy />
        <SizeBasedTriggeringPolicy size="10 MB"/>
      </Policies>
      <DefaultRolloverStrategy max="5"/>
    </RollingFile>
  </Appenders>
  <Loggers>
    <Root level="info">
      <AppenderRef ref="RollingFile"/>
    </Root>
  </Loggers>
</Configuration>
```

Notice that it's the same thing but without console output and I named it "log4j2.xml". Both are in the root folder of your classes (WEB-INF/classes) so how does Log4j knows which one to load? The answer is one parameter you have to pass to the VM of your development runtime server:

```
-Dlog4j.configurationFile=log4j2-dev.xml
```

This way, log4j will switch the loading file and in the production environment because without any parameter it will simply get the default file. You may be thinking that every application deployed in this server will be affected by this attribute because it is in the VM scope, yes and there are many other ways to have custom configurations on log4j 2, but I consider this as the simplest solution for a simple development environment, as well as non-invasive for your application because the default behavior is to get the production file.

To add this parameter in Eclipse environment, double click the server's name in the server's view, you will open the "Overview" page of your server, then in the General Information section click on "Open launch configuration" and you will get this dialog:

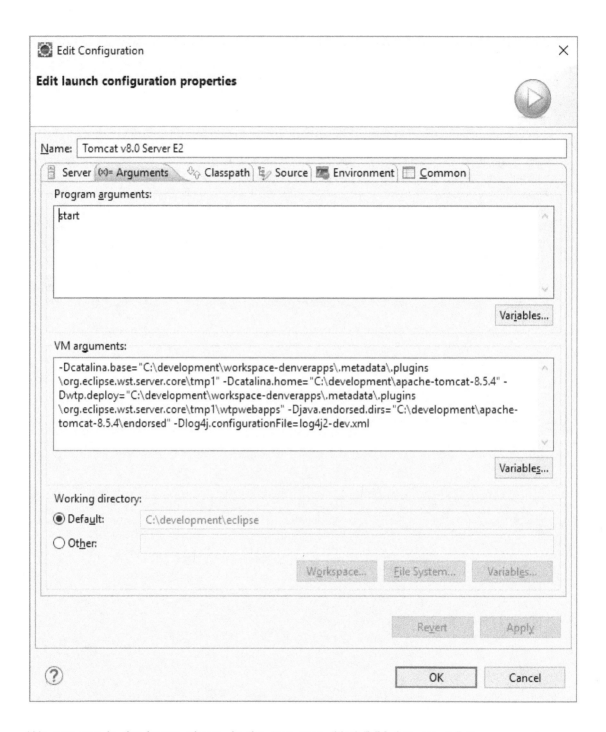

We can see in the image above, in the text area titled "VM Arguments" the parameter already added.

Context Path Initialization

Another useful initialization event to be captured by your application is the creation of the context path, as told at the beginning of this chapter Tomcat will create a mapping context to allow your application to be accessed, it is good to have it logged to check if your application was deployed as expected. The code snippet below shows one example to use:

```java
import javax.servlet.ServletContextEvent;
import javax.servlet.ServletContextListener;
import javax.servlet.annotation.WebListener;

import org.apache.logging.log4j.LogManager;
import org.apache.logging.log4j.Logger;

/**
 * @author Juliano Cassoli
 *
 */
@WebListener
public class AppContextInitializer implements
ServletContextListener {

    private static final Logger logger =
LogManager.getLogger(AppContextInitializer.class);

    /* (non-Javadoc)
     * @see
javax.servlet.ServletContextListener#contextDestroyed(javax.ser
vlet.ServletContextEvent)
     */
    @Override
    public void contextDestroyed(ServletContextEvent
contextEvent) {
        logger.info("Servlet context [" +
contextEvent.getServletContext().getContextPath()
                    + "] is closing. Goodbye.");
    }

    /* (non-Javadoc)
     * @see
javax.servlet.ServletContextListener#contextInitialized(javax.s
ervlet.ServletContextEvent)
     */
    @Override
    public void contextInitialized(ServletContextEvent
contextEvent) {

        logger.info("Application context initialized: " +
```

```
contextEvent.getServletContext().getContextPath());

        }

}
```

Maven dependencies

To have the servlets library in the class path but not been deployed in your server, because obviously the server already has this, see below:

```
<dependency>
    <groupId>javax.servlet</groupId>
    <artifactId>javax.servlet-api</artifactId>
    <version>3.1.0</version>
    <scope>provided</scope>
</dependency>
```

To have Log4j 2 integrated you have to use below:

```
<dependency>
        <groupId>org.apache.logging.log4j</groupId>
        <artifactId>log4j-api</artifactId>
        <version>2.6.2</version>
</dependency>
<dependency>
        <groupId>org.apache.logging.log4j</groupId>
        <artifactId>log4j-core</artifactId>
        <version>2.6.2</version>
</dependency>
<dependency>
    <groupId>org.apache.logging.log4j</groupId>
    <artifactId>log4j-web</artifactId>
    <version>2.6.2</version>
    <scope>runtime</scope>
</dependency>
```

And to have spring running you will have to add (all the dependencies are download automatically by maven, in case of `spring-context` for example, the modules `spring-core` and `spring-beans` are implicitly linked):

```
            <dependency>
                <groupId>org.springframework</groupId>
                <artifactId>spring-context</artifactId>
                <version>4.3.3.RELEASE</version>
            </dependency>

              <dependency>
                    <groupId>org.springframework</groupId>
                    <artifactId>spring-web</artifactId>
                    <version>4.3.3.RELEASE</version>
              </dependency>
```

This full example can be found a GitHub:

https://github.com/jucassoli/WebApplicationWithSpringAnnotationDrivenConfiguration/tree/master/Chapter2

Chapter 3. Configuration, DI and IoC

One of the main reasons you should adopt the Spring Framework is its support for Dependency Injection (DI) and Inversion of Control (IoC). When you are designing an application and starts dealing with decisions around creation of objects and therefore memory management, especially in web application environment where memory allocation can grow exponentially until a fast "out of memory" depending on your programming decisions upon user access, you will end up trying to create something to manage your business logic objects. Spring framework has an object manager at its heart, DI and IoC are not just features but they are a fundamental part of the framework, they provide a sophisticated programmatic mechanism of decoupling and implementation of the factory pattern, giving the developer the means to build the application around the concept of services.

Look at the introduction taken from the Spring Framework web site:

> The Spring Framework provides a comprehensive programming and configuration model for modern Java-based enterprise applications - on any kind of deployment platform. A key element of Spring is infrastructural support at the application level: Spring focuses on the "plumbing" of enterprise applications so that teams can focus on application-level business logic, without unnecessary ties to specific deployment environments.

In this chapter we are going to have a very simple configuration where our software parts will be represented as services using the annotations @Service or @Component, creating interfaces and giving the instantiation process to the framework, this way each time we need to have an object to call its methods we will make use of a mechanism of Spring.

First let's take a look of the initialization class, like the preceding chapter but now it does activate this mechanism by indicating Spring the package names to scan for its annotations:

```
import javax.servlet.ServletContext;
import javax.servlet.ServletException;

import org.apache.logging.log4j.LogManager;
import org.apache.logging.log4j.Logger;
import org.springframework.web.WebApplicationInitializer;
import org.springframework.web.context.ContextLoaderListener;
import
org.springframework.web.context.support.AnnotationConfigWebAppl
icationContext;

/**
```

```
 * @author Juliano Cassoli
 *
 */
public class MyAppInitializer implements
WebApplicationInitializer {

     private static final Logger logger =
LogManager.getLogger(MyAppInitializer.class);

     @Override
     public void onStartup(ServletContext servletContext)
throws ServletException {

          // Some useful information
          logger.info("Chapter 3 Example version 1.0.0");
          logger.info("OS: " + System.getProperty("os.name")
+ ", version " + System.getProperty("os.version")
               + ", Archtecture " +
System.getProperty("os.arch"));
          logger.info("Processors: " +
Runtime.getRuntime().availableProcessors());

          // Initiate Spring context and scan for services
annotated
          AnnotationConfigWebApplicationContext context = new
AnnotationConfigWebApplicationContext();
        context.setConfigLocation("com.wasadc.common.init");
        servletContext.addListener(new
ContextLoaderListener(context));

     }

}
```

We can see the code instantiating the class **AnnotationConfigWebApplicationContext** which is the implementation of the configuration for the web applications, it will scan the packages of a given string set with the method "**setConfigLocation**" and then register the Spring context listener.

At this moment Spring will initialize its Bean Manager engine, that will provide all DI and IoC. First it scans for @Configuration to load the classes providing methods for getting beans, as well as classes indicated with @Service and @Component to automatically link with references with @Autowire.

As you can see I first point Spring to my @Configuration class in the **setConfigLocation** method passing its specific package "`com.wasadc.common.init`". And then Spring will load all the rest of the annotations by reading `@ComponentScan`. It is just a matter of organization.

In this example we will explore two ways of obtaining the object that implements our service interface. Here is our configuration class:

```java
import org.apache.logging.log4j.LogManager;
import org.apache.logging.log4j.Logger;
import org.springframework.context.ApplicationEvent;
import org.springframework.context.ApplicationListener;
import org.springframework.context.annotation.Bean;
import org.springframework.context.annotation.Configuration;
import org.springframework.context.event.ContextClosedEvent;
import org.springframework.context.event.ContextRefreshedEvent;

import com.wasadc.calc.CalculationService;
import com.wasadc.calc.CalculationServiceIml;

/**
 * @author Juliano Cassoli
 *
 */
@Configuration
@ComponentScan(basePackages = "com.wasadc")
public class SpringApplicationInitConfig implements
ApplicationListener<ApplicationEvent> {

    private static final Logger logger =
LogManager.getLogger(SpringApplicationInitConfig.class);

    @Override
    public void onApplicationEvent(ApplicationEvent event) {
        // Bean Manager Started
        if(event instanceof ContextRefreshedEvent) {
            logger.info("Spring Bean Manager Started");
        }

        // Shutting down application
        if(event instanceof ContextClosedEvent) {
            logger.info("Spring context closed.");
        }
    }

    @Bean
    public CalculationService getCalculationService() {
        return new CalculationServiceIml();
    }
}
```

One way is to have a method annotated with @Bean which returns an object as a Bean within a FactoryBean, and this way you can implement any processing before returning the object and either control what class you will instantiate as the returning object. You can have an algorithm to choose what is going to be the right implementation of your service on a given situation.

The other way is to have the service implementation annotated with @Service (p.s. It would work with @Component too, spring gives you 2 annotations just to have an option to organize better your code). One thing worth mention in this case, you actually don't need to create interfaces (from Spring point of view) but it's a good practice and it will give you the power to control the instantiation by changing the class you annotate with `@Service` or `@Component`. Here is our example:

```java
/**
 * @author Juliano Cassoli
 *
 */
public interface MessageService {

      String createTextMessage(String name);

}
```

And then we have the implementation annotated with `@Service`:

```java
import org.springframework.stereotype.Service;

/**
 * @author Juliano Cassoli
 *
 */
@Service
public class MessageServiceImpl implements MessageService {

      /* (non-Javadoc)
       * @see
com.wasadc.text.MessageService#createTextMessage(java.lang.Stri
ng)
       */
      @Override
      public String createTextMessage(String name) {
            return "This is my message to " + name;
      }
```

```
    }
```

Adding something interesting to the Configuration class

As you can see the class also implements the interface ApplicationListener that it is not necessary to the @Configuration annotation but I decided to enrich this example to illustrate how can you evolve additional configuration to your application getting the events of starting and shutting down of the Bean Manager.

Spring Beans with Servlets

If you plan to use `@Autowire` to retrieve the service's object, the class where you use it must be "seen" by the Spring configuration, meaning that you have to put it in the context, by annotating it with `@Service, @component` or `@Configuration` (or annotated with `@Controller` as we will see later). But what if you need a simpler approach and want to get a service in a Servlet call? Remember that servlets loaded by the tomcat container are not in the Spring context (and aren`t in Bean Manager). The way to do it is by obtaining a `WebApplicationContext` calling `WebApplicationContextUtils` passing the Servlet context. Look at the example:

```java
import java.io.IOException;

import javax.servlet.ServletException;
import javax.servlet.annotation.WebServlet;
import javax.servlet.http.HttpServlet;
import javax.servlet.http.HttpServletRequest;
import javax.servlet.http.HttpServletResponse;

import org.springframework.web.context.WebApplicationContext;
import
org.springframework.web.context.support.WebApplicationContextUt
ils;

import com.wasadc.calc.CalculationService;
import com.wasadc.text.MessageService;

/**
 * @author Juliano Cassoli
 *
 */
@WebServlet(urlPatterns = { "/show" })
public class ShowMessageServlet extends HttpServlet {
```

```java
        private static final long serialVersionUID =
6621205430874548238L;

    @Override
    protected void doGet(HttpServletRequest request,
HttpServletResponse response) throws ServletException,
IOException {

        // Get spring context from the web application
context
        WebApplicationContext springContext =
WebApplicationContextUtils

    .getWebApplicationContext(getServletContext());

        // Obtain service instance
        MessageService mServ =
springContext.getBean(MessageService.class);
        CalculationService cServ =
springContext.getBean(CalculationService.class);

        String calcResult = "" + cServ.sum(2, 5);

        response.getWriter().append("Service responded:
").append(mServ.createTextMessage("John"))
                .append(", calc: ").append(calcResult);

    }


}
```

Accessing services or components with @Autowire

Instead of accessing the `WebApplicationContext` you can simply make use of `@Autowire`. The following code illustrates it.

```java
import org.springframework.beans.factory.annotation.Autowired;
import org.springframework.stereotype.Component;

import com.wasadc.calc.CalculationService;
import com.wasadc.text.MessageService;

/**
```

```
 * @author Juliano Cassoli
 *
 */
@Component
public class MessageCalculated {

    @Autowired
    private MessageService mServ;

    @Autowired
    private CalculationService cServ;

    public String getJoinedServices(String name, int a, int
b) {
            return "Message: " + mServ.createTextMessage(name)
+ ", sum=" + cServ.sum(a, b);
    }
}
```

This class marked with @Component will make use of the two services, at the time Spring instantiates MessageCalculated it fulfills the two private variables with the needed objects from the object manager. Again with a simple servlet example you can make use of this "component" just like you do with "service", see the following:

```
import javax.servlet.ServletException;
import javax.servlet.annotation.WebServlet;
import javax.servlet.http.HttpServlet;
import javax.servlet.http.HttpServletRequest;
import javax.servlet.http.HttpServletResponse;

import org.springframework.web.context.WebApplicationContext;
import
org.springframework.web.context.support.WebApplicationContextUt
ils;

/**
 * Servlet implementation class AnotherTextMessage
 */
@WebServlet("/testme")
public class AnotherTextMessage extends HttpServlet {

    private static final long serialVersionUID = 1L;


    /**
```

```
       * @see HttpServlet#doGet(HttpServletRequest request,
HttpServletResponse response)
       */
      protected void doGet(HttpServletRequest request,
HttpServletResponse response) throws ServletException,
IOException {

          WebApplicationContext springContext =
WebApplicationContextUtils

    .getWebApplicationContext(getServletContext());

          MessageCalculated serv =
springContext.getBean(MessageCalculated.class);


          response.getWriter().append("My message is
").append(serv.getJoinedServices("test", 5, 8));

      }

}
```

You can download and run the examples of this chapter accessing GitHub, here is the link:

https://github.com/jucassoli/WebApplicationWithSpringAnnotationDrivenConfiguration/tree/master/Chapter3

Chapter 4. Spring MVC

In the previous chapter we have used pure servlets to invoke services under Spring Bean Manager and respond to requests. But Spring has a feature destined to help you to build your application with the MVC pattern, through the @Controller and @RequestMapping annotations, offering a wide range of flexible handling methods. It not just allows you easily build your dispatching flow with JSPs but it's a very good helping hand to create RESTful Web sites and applications.

Maven

First of all, we will have to add the appropriate dependency to our POM:

```xml
<dependency>
    <groupId>org.springframework</groupId>
    <artifactId>spring-webmvc</artifactId>
    <version>4.3.3.RELEASE</version>
</dependency>

<dependency>
    <groupId>commons-fileupload</groupId>
    <artifactId>commons-fileupload</artifactId>
    <version>1.3.2</version>
</dependency>

<dependency>
    <groupId>com.fasterxml.jackson.core</groupId>
    <artifactId>jackson-core</artifactId>
    <version>2.8.3</version>
</dependency>

<dependency>
    <groupId>com.fasterxml.jackson.module</groupId>
    <artifactId>jackson-module-jaxb-
annotations</artifactId>
    <version>2.8.3</version>
</dependency>
```

The module commons-fileupload will give support for uploading files through controller mappings and the Jackson API is an efficient library to serialize or map Java objects to JSON and vice versa, it is used when controllers need to serialize objects to JSON as responses.

Configuring the DispatcherServlet

Go back to your initializer **MyAppInitializer**, now it must contain the dispatcher registration:

```java
import javax.servlet.ServletContext;
import javax.servlet.ServletException;
import javax.servlet.ServletRegistration;

import org.apache.logging.log4j.LogManager;
import org.apache.logging.log4j.Logger;
import org.springframework.web.WebApplicationInitializer;
import org.springframework.web.context.ContextLoaderListener;
import
org.springframework.web.context.support.AnnotationConfigWebAppl
icationContext;
import org.springframework.web.servlet.DispatcherServlet;

/**
 * @author Juliano Cassoli
 *
 */
public class MyAppInitializer implements
WebApplicationInitializer {

    private static final Logger logger =
LogManager.getLogger(MyAppInitializer.class);

    public static final String CONFIG_PACKAGE =
"com.wasadc.common.init";
    public static final String DISPATCHER_MAPPING = "/s/*";

    @Override
    public void onStartup(ServletContext servletContext)
throws ServletException {

        // Some useful information
        logger.info("Chapter 4 Example version 1.0.0");
        logger.info("OS: " + System.getProperty("os.name")
+ ", version " + System.getProperty("os.version")
            + ", Archtecture " +
System.getProperty("os.arch"));
        logger.info("Processors: " +
Runtime.getRuntime().availableProcessors());

        // Initiate Spring context and scan for services
annotated
        AnnotationConfigWebApplicationContext context = new
```

```
AnnotationConfigWebApplicationContext();
        context.setConfigLocation(CONFIG_PACKAGE);
        servletContext.addListener(new
ContextLoaderListener(context));

        // Dispatcher for all controller mappings
        ServletRegistration.Dynamic dispatcher =
servletContext.addServlet("DispatcherServlet",
                new DispatcherServlet(context));
        dispatcher.setLoadOnStartup(1);
        dispatcher.addMapping(DISPATCHER_MAPPING);
    }

}
```

The request mapping for the controllers will work quite the same as servlets do but in a second level. You have a mapping pattern that the server uses to invoke the servlet. In the case of controllers, you have to indicate the mapping that the server will pass all the requests to the framework and then it processes and decides what controller should respond to that request.

Notice we have a dispatcher mapping "/s/*" meaning that all requests the server receives with URL starting with /s/ will be passed to the controllers in the framework. This also means that you still can have servlets on your application, they will work if you avoid the "/s/".

Specific Configuration and Resolvers

To have better organization in the code we will have another configuration class, now specifically for the Web MVC mechanism, let's call it **WebMvcConfig** and remember, you can have as many as configuration classes as you want.

```
import org.springframework.context.annotation.Bean;
import org.springframework.context.annotation.Configuration;
import org.springframework.web.multipart.MultipartResolver;
import
org.springframework.web.multipart.commons.CommonsMultipartResol
ver;
import org.springframework.web.servlet.ViewResolver;
import
org.springframework.web.servlet.config.annotation.EnableWebMvc;
import
org.springframework.web.servlet.config.annotation.WebMvcConfigu
rerAdapter;
```

```java
import
org.springframework.web.servlet.view.InternalResourceViewResolv
er;

/**
 * @author Juliano Cassoli
 *
 */
@Configuration
@EnableWebMvc
public class WebMvcConfig extends WebMvcConfigurerAdapter {

    @Bean
    public MultipartResolver multipartResolver(){
            CommonsMultipartResolver multipartResolver = new
CommonsMultipartResolver();
        return multipartResolver;
    }

    @Bean
    public ViewResolver getViewResolver() {
            InternalResourceViewResolver resolver = new
InternalResourceViewResolver();
            resolver.setPrefix("/jsp/");
        resolver.setSuffix(".jsp");
        return resolver;
    }

    @Bean
    public MappingJackson2HttpMessageConverter
getHttpMessageConverter() {
            return new MappingJackson2HttpMessageConverter();
    }
}
```

In this configuration we have to put resolvers to work with our controllers, the first will process multipart requests for file uploads, the second will perform forward the processing thread to JSPs, with this configuration the View Resolver will find the file using this prefix and suffix, in other words, all files must have the JSP extension, and must be somewhere under the folder "/jsp". And the third is meant to provide serialization of objects to JSON format.

Forwarding to JSPs

Let's illustrate a forwarding to a JSP with a simple controller:

```java
import java.io.IOException;

import javax.servlet.ServletException;
import javax.servlet.http.HttpServletRequest;
import javax.servlet.http.HttpServletResponse;

import org.apache.logging.log4j.LogManager;
import org.apache.logging.log4j.Logger;
import org.springframework.stereotype.Controller;
import org.springframework.web.bind.annotation.RequestMapping;

/**
 * @author Juliano Cassoli
 *
 */
@Controller
public class MyHomePage {

    private static final Logger logger =
LogManager.getLogger(MyHomePage.class);

    @RequestMapping("/home")
    public String processShare(HttpServletRequest request,
            HttpServletResponse response) throws
ServletException, IOException {

        logger.info("process something");

        return "home/myHome";
    }

}
```

Like was mention before, annotating this class with @Controller will make the object part of the bean manager like any other service. The @RequestMapping annotation indicates that requests with "/s/home" (remember we have registered the dispatcher mapping as "/s/*") will be met by the method named "processShare" and notice that the request and response objects will be injected by the framework, just like a servlet method. As a result of returning the string, and have the View Resolver configured, it will be forwarded to a JSP file in "/jsp/home/myHome.jsp". The construction of the method that receives the request is very flexible, to see more possibilities refer to the Spring MVC documentation.

RESTful Web Service

To have our controller responding as a restful service, create a simple POJO (Plain Old Java Object) with the parameters you wish to be the constitution of the JSON response, like this one below:

```java
/**
 * @author Juliano Cassoli
 *
 */
public class MessageInfo {

    private String name;
    private String message;
    private int number;

    public String getName() {
        return name;
    }
    public void setName(String name) {
        this.name = name;
    }
    public String getMessage() {
        return message;
    }
    public void setMessage(String message) {
        this.message = message;
    }
    public int getNumber() {
        return number;
    }
    public void setNumber(int number) {
        this.number = number;
    }

}
```

Then you have to put it as a return from the method that responds to the request. See below:

```java
import org.apache.logging.log4j.LogManager;
import org.apache.logging.log4j.Logger;
import org.springframework.beans.factory.annotation.Autowired;
import org.springframework.stereotype.Controller;
import org.springframework.web.bind.annotation.RequestMapping;
import org.springframework.web.bind.annotation.ResponseBody;
```

```
import com.wasadc.text.MessageService;

/**
 * @author Juliano Cassoli
 *
 */
@Controller
public class MyRestMessageController {

    private static final Logger logger =
LogManager.getLogger(MyRestMessageController.class);

    @Autowired
    private MessageService mServ;

    @RequestMapping(value="/mymess", produces =
"application/json")
    @ResponseBody
    public MessageInfo processMessage() {

        String message =
mServ.createTextMessage("Richard");

        MessageInfo mi = new MessageInfo();
        mi.setMessage(message);
        mi.setName("John");
        mi.setNumber(13);

        logger.info("Got my message processed here");

        return mi;
    }
}
```

This way your response will be like this:

```
{"name":"John","message":"This is my message to
Richard","number":13}
```

As you can see there is a service been injected at the beginning, the MessageService, then the method to process the request annotated with @RequestMapping and @ResponseBody, indicating that the returning object will be converted to JSON with the appropriated http header response.

Let's consider a client application in a web browser, in our examples we have a javascript code that performs a request to this controller, look the file showMessage.jsp:

```
<!DOCTYPE html>
<html>
<head>
<script
src="https://ajax.googleapis.com/ajax/libs/jquery/3.1.1/jquery.
min.js"></script>
<meta http-equiv="Content-Type" content="text/html;
charset=ISO-8859-1">
<title>My Message</title>
</head>
<body>

<script>

$("document").ready(function() {

    $.ajax({
        method: "GET",
        dataType: "json",
        url: '<%=request.getContextPath()%>/s/mymess',
        success: function(data) {
            $("#msgNameContainer").text(data.name);
            $("#msgMessageContainer").text(data.message);
            $("#msgNumberContainer").text(data.number);
        },
        cache: false
    });

});

</script>

<p>Message test</p>

<p>This is a message to <span id="msgNameContainer"></span>,
saying <span id="msgMessageContainer"></span> with the
number <span id="msgNumberContainer"></span>
</p>

</body>
</html>
```

We use jQuery to perform the Ajax call to the controller and obtain the response as the "data" object. Notice that the names used as the properties of data are the same names as the POJO we created.

Uploading Files with Controllers

Almost every web application will end up having to handle file uploads, here we are going to see an example of a file upload been handled by a Spring Controller. Let`s start by analyzing the controller:

```java
import java.io.IOException;
import java.io.InputStream;

import javax.servlet.http.HttpServletRequest;
import javax.servlet.http.HttpServletResponse;

import org.apache.logging.log4j.LogManager;
import org.apache.logging.log4j.Logger;
import org.springframework.stereotype.Controller;
import org.springframework.web.bind.annotation.RequestMapping;
import org.springframework.web.bind.annotation.RequestParam;
import org.springframework.web.multipart.MultipartFile;

/**
 * @author Juliano Cassoli
 *
 */
@Controller
public class UpLoadController {

    private static final Logger logger =
LogManager.getLogger(UpLoadController.class);

    @RequestMapping(value="/upload")
    public String enterUpload() {

        return "upload/chooseToUp";
    }

    @RequestMapping(value="/save")
    public String
handleFileUpload(@RequestParam(value="comment") String comment,
        @RequestParam("file") MultipartFile file,
HttpServletRequest request,
                HttpServletResponse response){

        if (!file.isEmpty()) {
```

```java
                    String fileName = file.getOriginalFilename();
                    logger.info("file name: " + fileName);
                    logger.info("Comment: " + comment);

                    try {
                        InputStream is = file.getInputStream();
                        byte[] buffer = new byte[100_000];
                        int len;
                        while ((len = is.read(buffer)) != -1) {
                            logger.info("reading " + len + "
bytes");
                        }
                        is.close();


                    } catch (IOException e) {
                        // TODO Auto-generated catch block
                        e.printStackTrace();
                    }

            } else {
            return "upload/upFailed";
        }

            return "upload/upSucceeded";
    }

}
```

As you can see we have two mappings, the first just forwards to a JSP file called chooseToUp.jsp, this is the page with form and fields to perform the upload in the browser side. After selecting the file and hit the submit button, the browser will send the file on the second mapping (`"/save"`).

This example illustrates something more, think of how you indicate mappings on Servlets, you have one, or an array of mappings per Servlet (or class), and in the class you can have methods for different http types of requests, like get or post. But in the Spring Controller approach you may have a Controller (the class) having many mappings, each one been handled by a method. The Spring Controller can give you a good flexibility on how you organize the request-response flow.

This is the JSP used in this example to send the file back to the controller:

```html
<!DOCTYPE html>
<html>
```

```
<head>
<meta http-equiv="Content-Type" content="text/html;
charset=ISO-8859-1">
<title>Upload file test</title>
</head>
<body>

<form name="sendFileForm"
action="<%=request.getContextPath()%>/s/save"
     method="post" enctype="multipart/form-data">

     <p>File:<input type="file" name="file" ></p><br><br>
     <p>Comment: <input type="text" name="comment"
value=""></p>
     <p><input type="submit" name="submitMyFile"
value="Send"></p>
</form>

</body>
</html>
```

You can find a fully functional web application with the files printed here, access the link:

https://github.com/jucassoli/WebApplicationWithSpringAnnotationDrivenConfiguration/tree/master/Chapter4

Chapter 5. Persistence with Spring Data JPA and Hibernate

The persistence is an essential part of many systems, it is where you store and retrieve the all the information, and although NoSQL (and other types of) databases are getting more attention today, relational databases are still responsible for most of the manipulation and storage of information for web applications.

In this chapter we will be using Hibernate as our ORM (Object-relational mapping) engine, it means we are going to map classes (consequently objects), as a relational database model, and we are also will be using the Spring Data JPA to reduce our effort to build implementation of data manipulation through its sophisticated mechanism of repositories interfaces.

Here is an overview of what the example in this chapter is meant to provide:

- Read configuration access of the database and provide it to Spring
- Initialize Hibernate and integrate it with Spring Data JPA
- Create Entities that represents our domain
- Create our repository access interfaces
- Build our CRUD (Create Read Update Delete) code to manipulate the Data
- Access with Criteria API

Maven

Let's begin by listing our dependencies.

```xml
        <dependency>
            <groupId>org.springframework.data</groupId>
            <artifactId>spring-data-jpa</artifactId>
            <version>1.10.4.RELEASE</version>
        </dependency>

        <!-- Persistence API, Hibernate -->
        <dependency>

<groupId>org.hibernate.javax.persistence</groupId>
            <artifactId>hibernate-jpa-2.1-api</artifactId>
            <version>1.0.0.Final</version>
        </dependency>

        <dependency>
            <groupId>org.hibernate</groupId>
            <artifactId>hibernate-core</artifactId>
            <version>5.1.2.Final</version>
        </dependency>
```

```
        <dependency>
            <groupId>org.hibernate</groupId>
            <artifactId>hibernate-c3p0</artifactId>
            <version>5.1.2.Final</version>
        </dependency>

        <dependency>
            <groupId>org.hibernate</groupId>
            <artifactId>hibernate-
entitymanager</artifactId>
            <version>5.1.2.Final</version>
        </dependency>


        <!-- MySql Connector -->
        <dependency>
            <groupId>mysql</groupId>
            <artifactId>mysql-connector-java</artifactId>
            <version>6.0.4</version>
        </dependency>
```

As you can see the last dependency is the MySQL connector; it's our database of choice. If you want another RDBMS (Relational Database Management System) remember to check the availability on Hibernate, here you can find all Dialects present on version 5.1:

https://docs.jboss.org/hibernate/orm/5.1/javadocs/org/hibernate/dialect/package-summary.html

It is important to warn you that Spring 4.3.3 is not compatible with Hibernate versions higher then 5.1, if you want a newer Hibernate for any reason, you will have to check for other versions of Spring that supports it.

Reading Data Source Properties in the Initialization Class

At initialization time, the application will have to load the information that tells how to access the RDBMS and also other configuration parameters. The following code loads a properties file at the root of class path and sets a Property placeholder configuration of Spring. Here are our complete configuration class:

```
import java.io.IOException;
import java.io.InputStream;
import java.util.Properties;

import org.apache.logging.log4j.LogManager;
import org.apache.logging.log4j.Logger;
```

```java
import
org.springframework.beans.factory.config.PropertyPlaceholderCon
figurer;
import org.springframework.context.ApplicationEvent;
import org.springframework.context.ApplicationListener;
import org.springframework.context.annotation.Bean;
import org.springframework.context.annotation.ComponentScan;
import org.springframework.context.annotation.Configuration;
import org.springframework.context.event.ContextClosedEvent;
import org.springframework.context.event.ContextRefreshedEvent;

/**
 * @author Juliano Cassoli
 *
 */
@Configuration
@ComponentScan(basePackages = "com.wasadc")
public class SpringApplicationInitConfig implements
ApplicationListener<ApplicationEvent> {

    private static final Logger logger =
LogManager.getLogger(SpringApplicationInitConfig.class);

    public static final String PERSISTENCE_FILE_NAME = "data-
source.properties";

    @Override
    public void onApplicationEvent(ApplicationEvent event) {
        // Bean Manager Started
        if(event instanceof ContextRefreshedEvent) {
            logger.info("Spring Bean Manager Started");
        }

        // Shutting down application
        if(event instanceof ContextClosedEvent) {
            logger.info("Spring context closed.");
        }
    }

    @Bean
    public static PropertyPlaceholderConfigurer
getPropertyPlaceholderConfigurer(){

        InputStream is =
SpringApplicationInitConfig.class.getClassLoader()

    .getResourceAsStream(PERSISTENCE_FILE_NAME);
```

```
            PropertyPlaceholderConfigurer ppc = null;
            try {
                  ppc = new PropertyPlaceholderConfigurer();

                  Properties propsToPass = new Properties();
                  propsToPass.load(is);
                  ppc.setProperties(propsToPass);
                  ppc.setIgnoreUnresolvablePlaceholders(false);

            } catch (IOException e) {
                  // TODO Auto-generated catch block
                  e.printStackTrace();
            }

            return ppc;
      }

}
```

You must be wondering about what this pp class means, it will be explained later in this chapter, just keep in mind now that this implementation allows you to have properties file stored in another place like user home, just changing where you get the file, as a consequence, for example, you can have specific configuration for production and development environment.

Here goes what tells our application all about database access, the properties file **data-source.properties**:

```
# database configuration

# Database connection and authentication
jdbc.driverClassName=com.mysql.cj.jdbc.Driver
jdbc.url=jdbc:mysql://localhost:3306/test?useSSL=false&useJDBCC
ompliantTimezoneShift=true&serverTimezone=UTC
jdbc.schema=
jdbc.username=root
jdbc.password=a

# Spring Data JPA
jpa.database.name=MYSQL

# Hibernate Configuration
hibernate.dialect=org.hibernate.dialect.MySQLDialect

hibernate.show_sql=true
```

```
hibernate.format_sql=false
hibernate.use_sql_comments=false
hibernate.hbm2ddl.auto=update
hibernate.generate_statistics=false

# Connection Pool
hibernate.c3p0.acquireIncrement=1
hibernate.c3p0.min_size=10
hibernate.c3p0.max_size=95
hibernate.c3p0.max_statements=45
hibernate.c3p0.max_idletime=120
```

You will notice there are 4 section, the first one are specific properties related to the access of the database, they begin with "jdbc", it will be used basically to create the Data Source object that will compose the connection pool. The second is the name of the database system to the Spring JPA mechanism. The third and fourth are hibernate and connection pool configuration properties, you will find extensive documentation about them in the Hibernate web site.

Persistence Configuration Class

We are now going to dive in to a specific configuration class, one with only persistence related configuration (for organization purposes, of course you can put everything in one configuration class but it's easier to manage well organized classes), It's a quite long class so instead of writing everything down on a long "code quote", we are going to build it step by step. First consider the class with the appropriate annotations:

```
import java.beans.PropertyVetoException;
import java.util.Properties;

import javax.persistence.EntityManagerFactory;
import javax.sql.DataSource;

import org.apache.logging.log4j.LogManager;
import org.apache.logging.log4j.Logger;
import org.springframework.beans.factory.annotation.Autowired;
import org.springframework.beans.factory.annotation.Value;
import org.springframework.context.annotation.Bean;
import org.springframework.context.annotation.Configuration;
import
org.springframework.data.jpa.repository.config.EnableJpaReposit
ories;
import
org.springframework.orm.jpa.AbstractEntityManagerFactoryBean;
```

```
import org.springframework.orm.jpa.JpaTransactionManager;
import
org.springframework.orm.jpa.LocalContainerEntityManagerFactoryB
ean;
import org.springframework.orm.jpa.vendor.Database;
import
org.springframework.orm.jpa.vendor.HibernateJpaVendorAdapter;
import
org.springframework.transaction.annotation.EnableTransactionMan
agement;

import com.mchange.v2.c3p0.ComboPooledDataSource;

/**
 * @author Juliano Cassoli
 *
 */
@Configuration
@EnableJpaRepositories(basePackages="com.wasadc.domain")
@EnableTransactionManagement
public class PersistenceConfiguration {

}
```

The @Configuration must be present of course or it wouldn't be scanned as a configuration class. Then we have the indication to enable the JPA Repositories mechanisms, indicating the package where to scan for the Repository interfaces. And finally an indication that we want to enable the annotated transaction management.

Now we are ready to add body to the class, so we begin with some constants that will be used in mechanisms that will be later explained; and the variables that will be fulfilled by the `PropertyPlaceholderConfigurer` mechanism (remember we have started the `PropertyPlaceholderConfigurer` Bean earlier in our initialization class, now spring will use it to pass values to these variables).

```
    private static final Logger logger =
LogManager.getLogger(PersistenceConfiguration.class);

    public static final String HIBERNATE_LOCAL_SESSION_SCAN =
"com.wasadc";
    public static final String DOMAIN_ENTITY_SCAN =
"com.wasadc.domain";

    @Value("${jdbc.driverClassName}") private String
driverClassName;
```

```
@Value("${jdbc.url}") private String url;
@Value("${jdbc.schema}") private String schema;
@Value("${jdbc.username}") private String username;
@Value("${jdbc.password}") private String password;

@Value("${hibernate.dialect}") private String
hibernateDialect;
@Value("${hibernate.show_sql}") private String
hibernateShowSql;
@Value("${hibernate.format_sql}") private String
hibernateFormatSql;
@Value("${hibernate.use_sql_comments}") private String
hibernateCommentSql;
@Value("${hibernate.hbm2ddl.auto}") private String
hibernateHbm2ddlAuto;

@Value("${hibernate.c3p0.acquireIncrement}") private
String hibernateC3P0AcquireIncrement;
@Value("${hibernate.c3p0.min_size}") private String
hibernateC3P0MinSize;
@Value("${hibernate.c3p0.max_size}") private String
hibernateC3P0MaxSize;
@Value("${hibernate.c3p0.max_idletime}") private String
hibernateC3P0MaxIdleTime;
@Value("${hibernate.c3p0.max_statements}") private String
hibernateC3P0MaxStatements;

@Value("${jpa.database.name}") private String
databaseName;
```

Now that we have all the necessary properties. Let's create a method annotated with @Bean to provide the Data Source for the connection pool:

```
@Bean()
public javax.sql.DataSource getDataSource() {

    ComboPooledDataSource ds = new
ComboPooledDataSource();

    try {
        ds.setDriverClass(driverClassName);
        ds.setJdbcUrl(url);
        ds.setUser(username);
        ds.setPassword(password);
```

```
        ds.setAcquireIncrement(Integer.parseInt(hibernateC3P0Acqu
ireIncrement));

        ds.setMinPoolSize(Integer.parseInt(hibernateC3P0MinSize))
;

        ds.setMaxPoolSize(Integer.parseInt(hibernateC3P0MaxSize))
;

        ds.setMaxIdleTime(Integer.parseInt(hibernateC3P0MaxIdleTi
me));

        ds.setMaxStatementsPerConnection(Integer.parseInt(hiberna
teC3P0MaxStatements));

            } catch (NumberFormatException |
PropertyVetoException e) {
                logger.error("Could not create DataSource: " +
e.getMessage());
            }

        return ds;
    }
```

No secrets about it, the method talks by itself, it creates an instance of the DataSource that will populates our connection pool. Next, we need to provide the Bean that loads the Hibernate properties to have Spring able to run it:

```
    @Bean
    public Properties getHibernateProperties() {
        Properties properties = new Properties();
        properties.put("hibernate.dialect", hibernateDialect);
        properties.put("hibernate.show_sql", hibernateShowSql);
        properties.put("hibernate.format_sql",
hibernateFormatSql);
        properties.put("hibernate.use_sql_comments",
hibernateCommentSql);
        properties.put("hibernate.hbm2ddl.auto",
hibernateHbm2ddlAuto);
        if(schema != null && !schema.isEmpty()){
            properties.put("hibernate.default_schema", schema);

        }
            properties.put("sequence", "custom_hibernate_seq");
```

```
    return properties;
}
```

Next, we have to set the Entity Manager Factory to Spring JPA with Hibernate Adapter, so spring will be able to use its Entity Manager to perform the queries.

```
    @Bean
    @Autowired
    public AbstractEntityManagerFactoryBean
entityManagerFactory(DataSource dataSource) {

        HibernateJpaVendorAdapter vendorAdapter = new
HibernateJpaVendorAdapter();

        vendorAdapter.setDatabase(Database.valueOf(databaseName))
;
        vendorAdapter.setGenerateDdl(true);

        LocalContainerEntityManagerFactoryBean factory = new
LocalContainerEntityManagerFactoryBean();
        factory.setJpaVendorAdapter(vendorAdapter);
        factory.setPackagesToScan(DOMAIN_ENTITY_SCAN);
        factory.setDataSource(dataSource);
        factory.setJpaProperties(getHibernateProperties());

        return factory;
    }
```

And finally we need to setup the transaction manager. This is a simple transaction manager approach and it is appropriate for applications that use a single JPA EntityManagerFactory for transactional data access.

```
    @Bean
    @Autowired
    public JpaTransactionManager
transactionManager(EntityManagerFactory emf) {
        if(emf==null) return null;
        JpaTransactionManager tm = new JpaTransactionManager();
        tm.setEntityManagerFactory(emf);
        return tm;
    }
```

If you need a more complex mechanism of transaction you should look for JtaTransactionManager, which is appropriate for handling distributed transactions, i.e. transactions that span multiple resources, and for controlling transactions on application server resources (e.g. JDBC DataSources available in JNDI) in general.

Creating an Entity class

Let's move forward and create our Entity class that will represent the data structure we need to store. To have an easy understanding of our example, consider this very simple employee model:

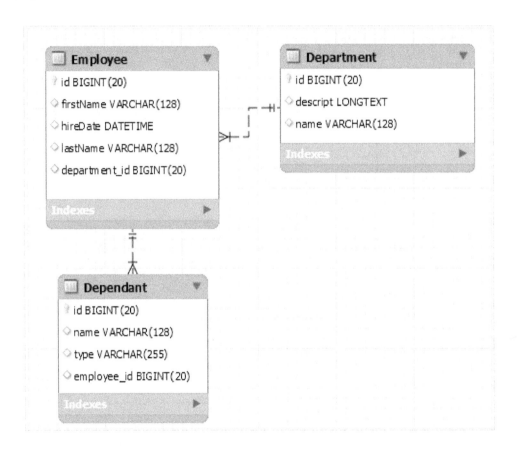

In its relational model, the Entity Employee has a numeric Id, which is its primary key, first and last name as String properties, a hire date, and it belongs to a Department, indicated by the department Id. You can see as well that we can have departments associated with many employees, and one Employee may have zero or many Dependents, like a child or a spouse. Given this model, let's create our Entity class:

```
import java.util.Calendar;
```

```java
import java.util.List;

import javax.persistence.Column;
import javax.persistence.Entity;
import javax.persistence.GeneratedValue;
import javax.persistence.GenerationType;
import javax.persistence.Id;
import javax.persistence.ManyToOne;
import javax.persistence.OneToMany;
import javax.persistence.Temporal;
import javax.persistence.TemporalType;

/**
 * @author Juliano Cassoli
 *
 */
@Entity
public class Employee {

    @Id
    @GeneratedValue(strategy=GenerationType.AUTO)
    private Long id;

    @Column(length=128, nullable=false)
    private String firstName;

    @Column(length=128, nullable=false)
    private String lastName;

    @Temporal(TemporalType.TIMESTAMP)
    private Calendar hireDate;

    @ManyToOne
    private Department department;

    @OneToMany(mappedBy="employee", orphanRemoval=true)
    private List<Dependant> dependants;


    public Long getId() {
        return id;
    }

    public void setId(Long id) {
        this.id = id;
    }

    public String getFirstName() {
```

```java
            return firstName;
    }

    public void setFirstName(String firstName) {
        this.firstName = firstName;
    }

    public String getLastName() {
        return lastName;
    }

    public void setLastName(String lastName) {
        this.lastName = lastName;
    }

    public Calendar getHireDate() {
        return hireDate;
    }

    public void setHireDate(Calendar hireDate) {
        this.hireDate = hireDate;
    }

    public Department getDepartment() {
        return department;
    }

    public void setDepartment(Department department) {
        this.department = department;
    }

    public List<Dependant> getDependants() {
        return dependants;
    }

    public void setDependants(List<Dependant> dependants) {
        this.dependants = dependants;
    }


}
```

In this Class we are telling Hibernate to have auto generation values for the Id, defining length for the String properties - they must not be null -, the hire date as a temporal type, a many-to-one relationship with department, meaning we can have many employees in one department and one employee with many dependents. See the Entity Department below:

```java
import java.util.List;

import javax.persistence.Column;
import javax.persistence.Entity;
import javax.persistence.GeneratedValue;
import javax.persistence.GenerationType;
import javax.persistence.Id;
import javax.persistence.OneToMany;

/**
 * @author Juliano Cassoli
 *
 */
@Entity
public class Department {

    @Id
    @GeneratedValue(strategy=GenerationType.AUTO)
    private Long id;

    @Column(length=128, nullable=false)
    private String name;

    @Column(length=2048)
    private String descript;

    @OneToMany(mappedBy="department")
    private List<Employee> employees;


    public Long getId() {
        return id;
    }

    public void setId(Long id) {
        this.id = id;
    }

    public String getName() {
        return name;
    }

    public void setName(String name) {
        this.name = name;
    }

    public String getDescript() {
        return descript;
```

```
        }

        public void setDescript(String descript) {
                this.descript = descript;
        }

        public List<Employee> getEmployees() {
                return employees;
        }

        public void setEmployees(List<Employee> employees) {
                this.employees = employees;
        }


}
```

And finally the Entity Dependant:

```
import javax.persistence.Column;
import javax.persistence.Entity;
import javax.persistence.EnumType;
import javax.persistence.Enumerated;
import javax.persistence.GeneratedValue;
import javax.persistence.GenerationType;
import javax.persistence.Id;
import javax.persistence.ManyToOne;

/**
 * @author Juliano Cassoli
 *
 */
@Entity
public class Dependant {

        @Id
        @GeneratedValue(strategy=GenerationType.AUTO)
        private Long id;

        @Column(length=128, nullable=false)
        private String name;

        @Enumerated(EnumType.STRING)
        private DependantType type;

        @ManyToOne
```

```java
        private Employee employee;


        public Long getId() {
                return id;
        }

        public void setId(Long id) {
                this.id = id;
        }

        public String getName() {
                return name;
        }

        public void setName(String name) {
                this.name = name;
        }

        public DependantType getType() {
                return type;
        }

        public void setType(DependantType type) {
                this.type = type;
        }

        public Employee getEmployee() {
                return employee;
        }

        public void setEmployee(Employee employee) {
                this.employee = employee;
        }

}
```

We are using the Dependant type as an Enum and to specify that we want Hibernate to store its String representation we need to annotate with @Enumerated(EnumType.STRING). See the definition below:

```java
public enum DependantType {
     SPOUSE, CHILD;
}
```

CRUD for the Employee Example

After defining the Entities, we will create the CRUD interfaces, which are goal of Spring Data repository abstraction. Take a look at the explanation found at Spring web site (http://docs.spring.io/spring-data/jpa/docs/current/reference/html/#repositories):

> The central interface in Spring Data repository abstraction is Repository (probably not that much of a surprise). It takes the domain class to manage as well as the id type of the domain class as type arguments. This interface acts primarily as a marker interface to capture the types to work with and to help you to discover interfaces that extend this one. The CrudRepository provides sophisticated CRUD functionality for the entity class that is being managed.

I personally prefer to use the interface `PagingAndSortingRepository` that adds additional methods to ease paginated access to entities. See below:

```java
import
org.springframework.data.repository.PagingAndSortingRepository;

import com.wasadc.domain.Employee;

/**
 * @author Juliano Cassoli
 *
 */
public interface EmployeeRepository extends
PagingAndSortingRepository<Employee, Long> {

    long countByDepartmentId(Long id);

}
```

You don't need to implement or create any additional method on your interface because there are many methods inherited from `PagingAndSortingRepository`, all the basic operations like find all registers, save new register, update existing, they are all part of Spring interface. But as you can see there is a method in our interface, called "countByDepartmentId", and that's where the magic happens, you will not implement this method, Spring will do, at the application startup time and based on the name you gave to it. So, the implementation of this method will count all the Employees associated with Department having the given Id.

Just to illustrate, we could get the same results if we substitute the "Long Id" by "Department dep", and take the "Id" from the name, instead of counting the results using the

Id of the Department, Spring would use the object Department. You could get a list of Employees if you have a method starting with "find" instead of "count", see below:

```
Iterable<Employee> findByDepartmentId(Long id);
```

In fact, there is a whole world of ways to use this feature, I am not going any further with it in this book, because Spring has it very well documented, my intention is get you started, up and running with the basics and then you can evolve.

Here goes a Controller snippet of how it could get a list of employees:

```
    @RequestMapping("/listEmployee")
    public ModelAndView listEmployee(HttpServletRequest
request,
                HttpServletResponse response) throws
ServletException, IOException {

        Iterable<Employee> employeeList = empRep.findAll();

        return new ModelAndView("employee/listEmployee",
"mylist", employeeList);
    }
```

Accessing with Criteria API

Using Spring Data JPA does not invalidates you to use the Criteria API. With the same configuration here is an example on how to perform the same operation but using Criteria API, this code is part of a Controller and lists all Departments, look:

```
    @RequestMapping("/listDepartment")
    public ModelAndView listDepartment(HttpServletRequest
request,
                HttpServletResponse response) throws
ServletException, IOException {

        CriteriaBuilder cbuilder = em.getCriteriaBuilder();
        CriteriaQuery<Department> query =
cbuilder.createQuery(Department.class);
        Root<Department> from =
query.from(Department.class);

        TypedQuery<Department> typedQuery =
```

```
em.createQuery(query);
         List<Department> resultList =
typedQuery.getResultList();

         return new ModelAndView("employee/listDepartment",
"allDepartment", resultList);
     }
```

This entire application, like the chapters before, can be downloaded at:

https://github.com/jucassoli/WebApplicationWithSpringAnnotationDrivenConfiguration/tree/master/Chapter5

Chapter 6. JMX and Managed Beans

In this chapter we will see how to manage attributes and operations of your application, not just for debugging purposes but to monitor the application's performance in production environment if you wish. Java Management Extensions (JMX) is a Java technology that lets you implement named objects - called MBeans (Management Beans) for your application, so you can manage resources creating indicators, or attributes, and even invoke methods on your services. This is done simply by connecting a MBeans client to the VM running your application.

If you are working with tomcat locally in your development environment, connecting to your application is straight forward. In Windows environment, you just have to point your client to the VM process running your tomcat and voilà. If you want to connect it remotely its necessary to enable JMX access in Tomcat, you will have to consider port available, SSL connection, authentication and authorization. In this case it's better to take a look at the Tomcat documentation:

https://tomcat.apache.org/tomcat-8.0-doc/monitoring.html

Using the Oracle VisualVM as the client

Oracle provides a tool called VisualVM, it can be found on your java installation folder, in my case it is "C:\Program Files\Java\jdk1.8.0_101\bin\jvisualvm.exe". We will be using it to access our MBeans provided by the application, so let's start by properly configuring the tool. The VisualVM application will not display your MBeans until you install a plugin, so after execute the application, go to `Tools -> Plugins`, as you see here:

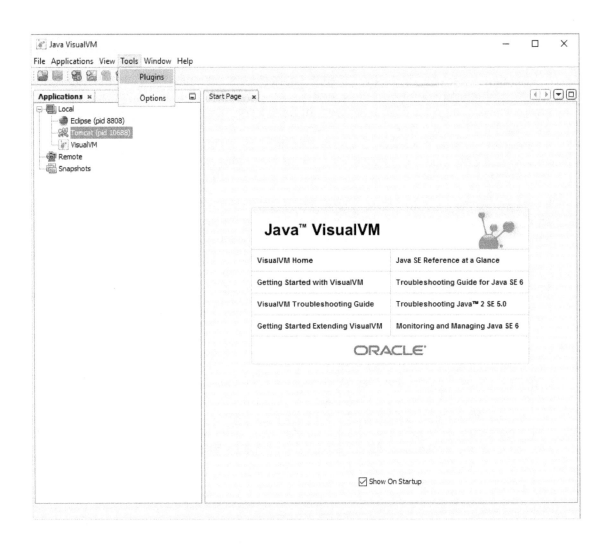

Then you must select and install the VM-MBeans plugin as shown here:

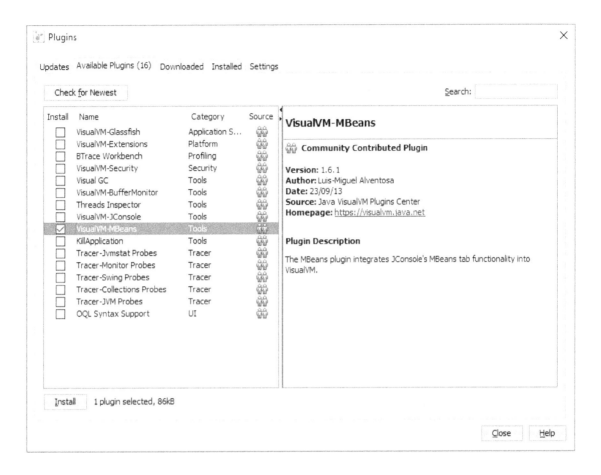

Application Configuration at Initialization

In the application code, we first have to put a Bean declaration in our initialization class, it's the Spring's exporter mechanism that will scan for our annotated MBeans:

```java
/**
 * MBean exporter
 *
 * @return
 */
@Bean
public AnnotationMBeanExporter getMBeanExporter() {
        AnnotationMBeanExporter mbean = new
AnnotationMBeanExporter();
        mbean.setAutodetect(true);
        return mbean;
}
```

Service Monitored and Managed

Annotation our service with @ManagedResource is enough to activate the Managed Bean. Each method of your service you wish to monitor or provide an action can be annotated like the example below:

```java
import org.springframework.jmx.export.annotation.ManagedMetric;
import
org.springframework.jmx.export.annotation.ManagedOperation;
import
org.springframework.jmx.export.annotation.ManagedResource;
import org.springframework.jmx.support.MetricType;
import org.springframework.stereotype.Service;

/**
 * @author Juliano Cassoli
 *
 */
@Service
@ManagedResource(objectName = "MyApp:name=MessageService")
public class MessageServiceImpl implements MessageService {

    private volatile long callCount;

    private volatile boolean interruptCount;

    /* (non-Javadoc)
     * @see
com.wasadc.text.MessageService#createTextMessage(java.lang.Stri
ng)
     */
    @Override
    public String createTextMessage(String name) {
        if (!interruptCount) callCount++;
        return "This is my message to " + name;
    }

    @ManagedMetric(unit="Messages", description = "Quantity",
metricType=MetricType.COUNTER)
    public long getServiceCallCount() {
        return callCount;
    }

    @ManagedOperation(description = "Interrupt the count")
    public void interruptCount() {
        interruptCount = true;
    }
```

```
        @ManagedOperation(description = "Resume the count")
        public void resumeCount() {
              interruptCount = false;
        }

        @ManagedOperation(description = "Reset the count")
        public void resetCounter() {
              callCount = 0;
        }


}
```

To monitor your application just select it in the VisualVM, with the name you configured in your service class. In our example just select "MyApp" and you can get the indicator's instant value (and even get it over time graphically if you double click the field), as well as all operations we have annotated, like shown below:

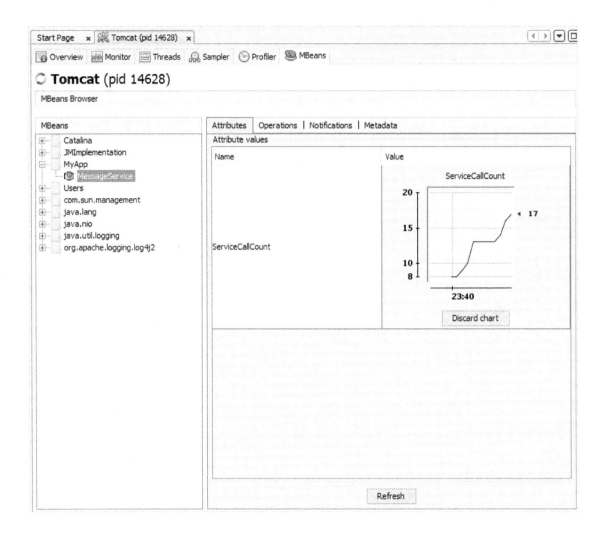

This chapter's full example application can be found at:

https://github.com/jucassoli/WebApplicationWithSpringAnnotationDrivenConfiguration/tree/master/Chapter6